SPRING IN JAPAN

WOODBLOCK PRINTS BY HOKUSAI, HIROSHIGE AND OTHER ARTISTS

I0418846

Spring in Japan

Woodblock Prints by Hokusai, Hiroshige and Other Artists

Jocelyn Bouquillard

PRESTEL
MUNICH · LONDON · NEW YORK

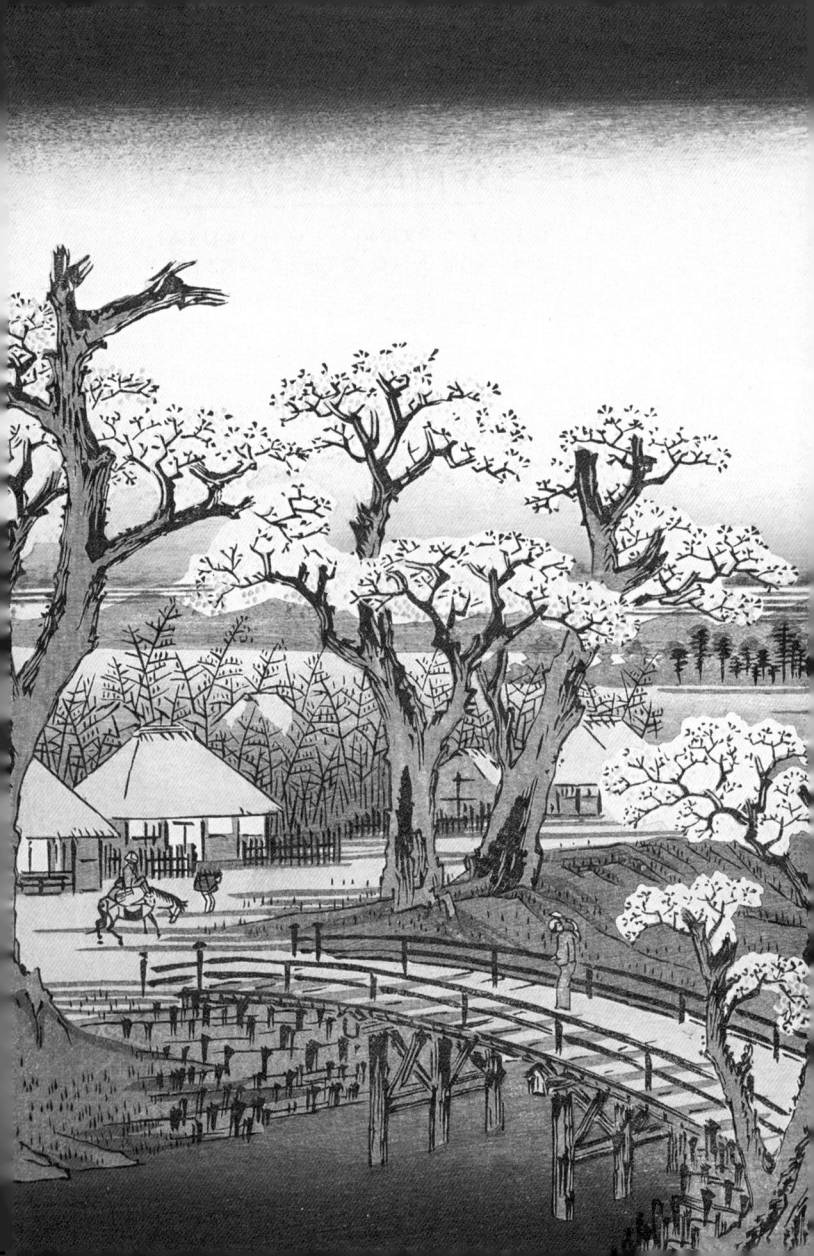

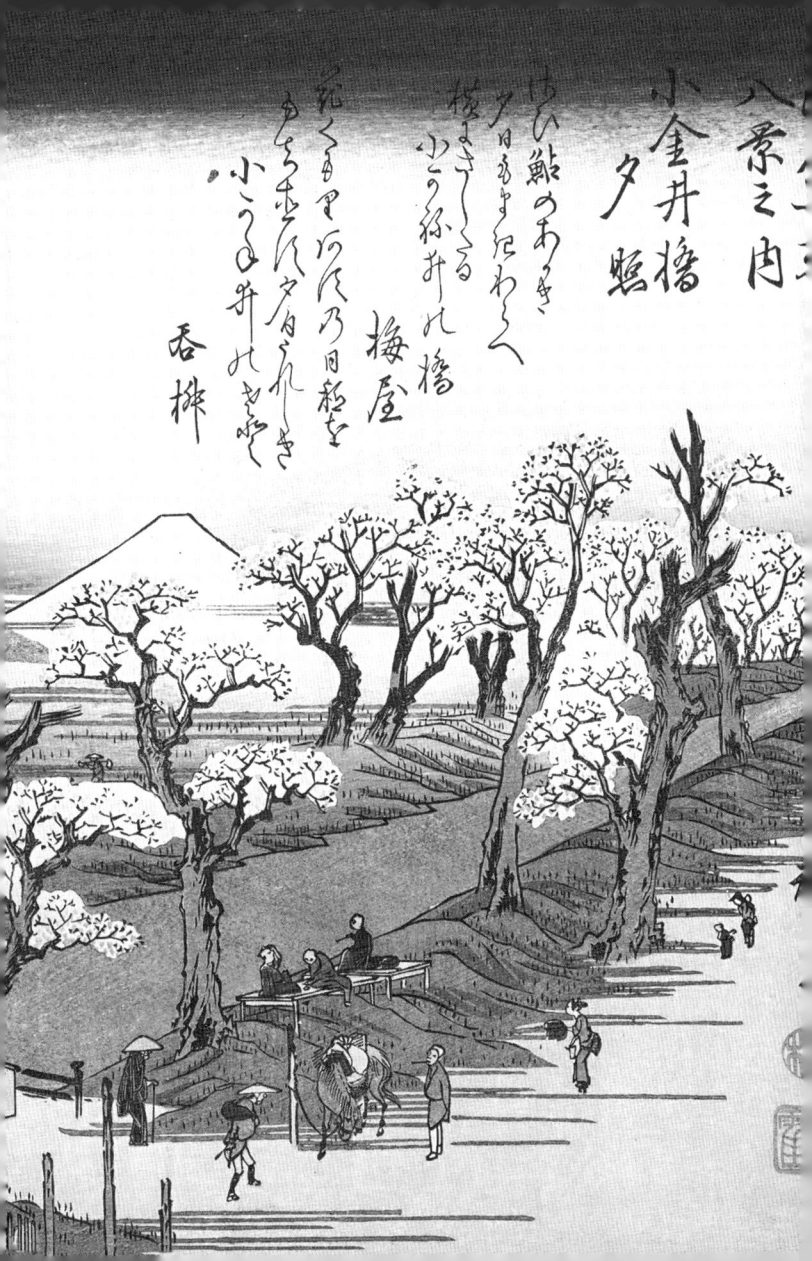

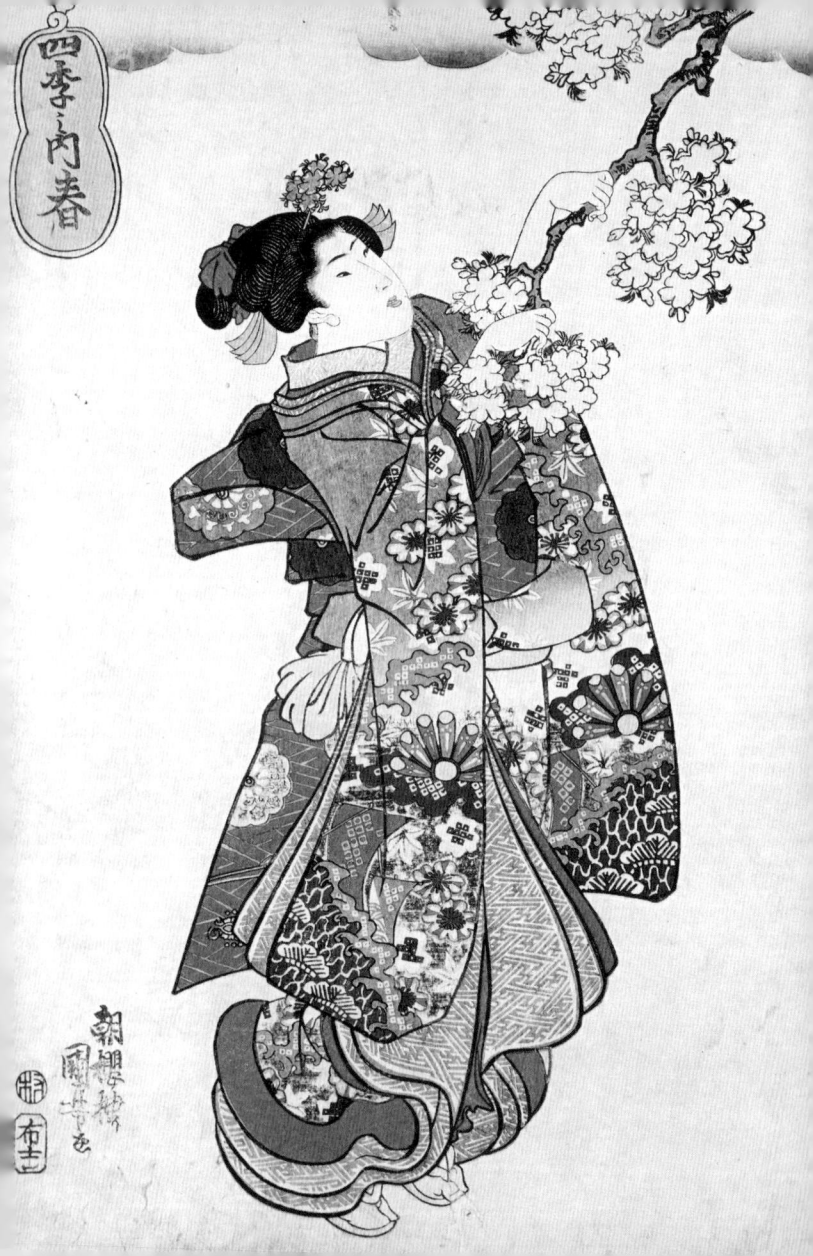

Exalted in both poetry and painting, springtime is one of the greatest sources of inspiration in the world of Japanese printmaking. "Images of the floating world" (*ukiyo-e*) celebrate this season when nature renews itself, with lush landscapes and blooming flower gardens echoing with birdsong. This ephemeral world, which is increasingly threatened today, has been immortalised at a time when one could still enjoy and live in harmony with a pristine natural environment, embracing the change of seasons.

Representations of springtime evoke the season's festive and joyful atmosphere, while also reminding us of the fragility of life and the fleeting pleasures it offers. This recurring theme is indeed one of the favourite subjects of *ukiyo-e*, which mainly focuses on depictions of nature and everyday life. Displaying particular sensitivity to the changes in the weather, to the cycle of the seasons and fleeting moments, the masters of Japanese printmaking embraced an approach that was both aesthetic and philosophical for the depiction of nature's ephemeral spectacle and cyclical rebirth. They worshipped cherry blossoms, the emblematic symbol of springtime in Japan, and produced series of prints devoted to flowers and birds (*kacho-ga*) that underlined the brevity of existence, while meditating on the precarious nature of beauty, thus inviting viewers to reflect with melancholy on the passing of time.

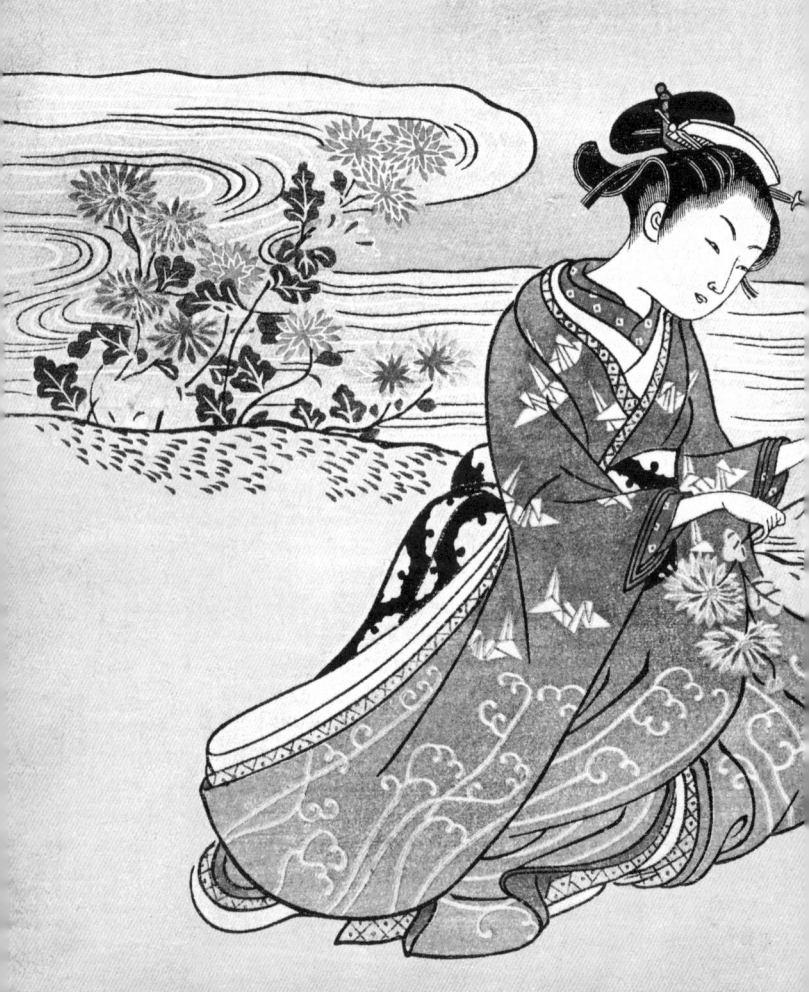

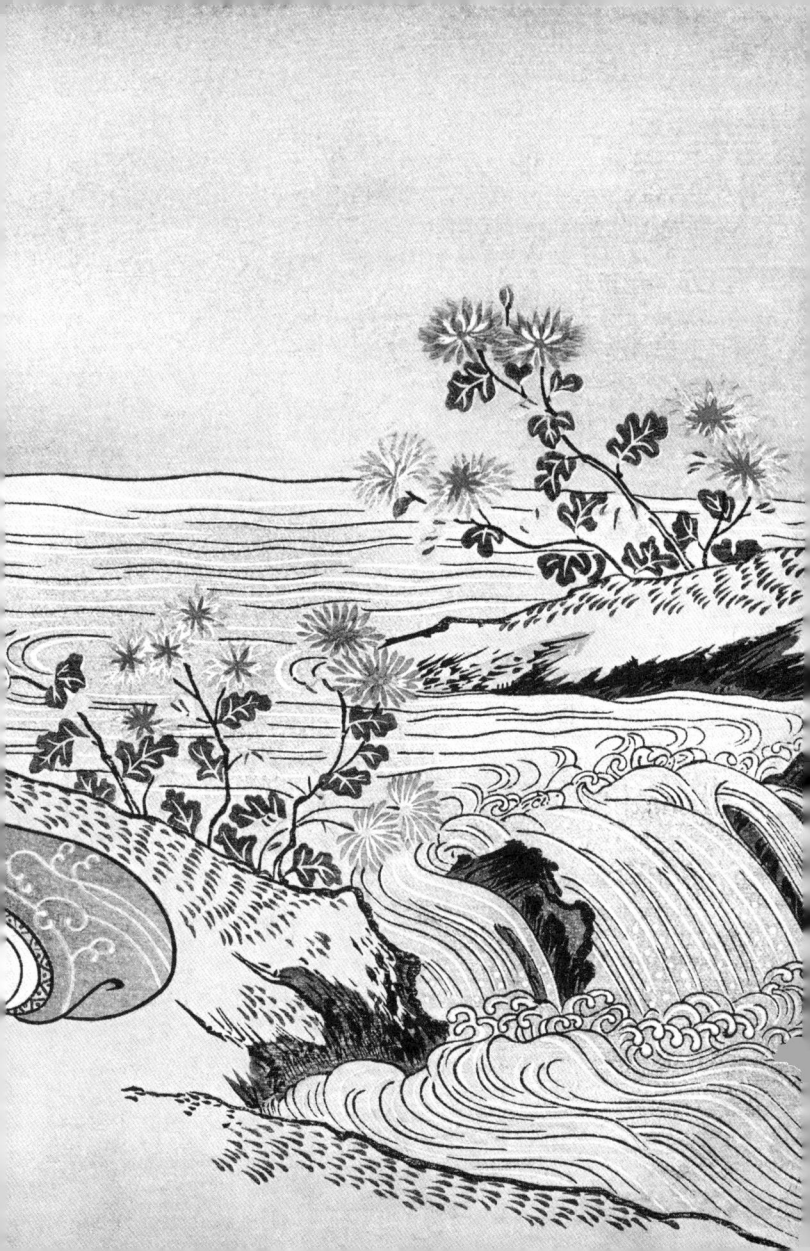

Shunga (images of springtime) and kimonos with springtime-inspired motifs

Traditionally, until the early 19th century, these prints were devoted to the pleasure districts of Edo (Tokyo's former name), its courtesans, geishas and actors. These images would often feature elegantly dressed figures strolling beneath flowering branches in verdant parks. Women dressed in light, colourful kimonos decorated with floral motifs, sometimes holding an umbrella or a fan, are depicted in springtime scenes of everyday life (plates 17, 18, 22, 23, 24, 27, 41, 42, 43, 46, 48, 52, 59, 61, 62, 63, 65, 67).

Suzuki Harunobu and Utagawa Kuniyoshi highlight the beauty of women, capturing their elegance in their springtime clothes. In their series entitled *Beauties of the Floating World Compared to Flowers* (pl. 65) and *The Five Flowers of Edo*, they depict women, associating them with different flowers, some of which evoke springtime, such as irises and plum, cherry and peach blossoms.

Erotic prints, a genre that was particularly prolific in Japan during the Edo period, were widely appreciated and distributed throughout the eighteenth century. These are known as *shunga*, which literally translates to "images of springtime", the season's gentle conditions being conducive to such intimate effusions. Sensual scenes, sometimes depicted in a humorous fashion, embody this call to enjoy the present moment, fleeting pleasures and ephemeral moments of happiness. Open kimonos exposing the protagonists' bodies are often adorned with spring motifs, as illustrated by this print by Harunobu (pl. 67), where the lovers are surrounded by flowers, symbolically representing the woman being voluptuously disrobed.

Fukei-ga (landscape prints) and *meisho-e* (views of famous places)

Springtime is particularly celebrated in landscape prints (*fukei-ga*). This new genre emerged in the 19th century, under the impetus of Katsushika

Hokusai and Utagawa Hiroshige, who renewed the traditional themes characteristic of *ukiyo-e*. At the time, these prints were confronted with a series of increasingly strict censorship edicts, which targeted the artists' favourite topics and restricted their freedom to produce *shunga* and portraits of courtesans and theatre actors.

In the 1830s, Hokusai and Hiroshige published two emblematic series; *Thirty-six Views of Mount Fuji*, for the former, and *The Fifty-three Stations of the Tōkaidō*, for the latter. Both were met with great interest. These series resonated with the aspirations of Japanese society, which was passionate about nature and travels across the archipelago. Landscapes, which had until then been relegated to the background of *ukiyo-e* prints, were now represented in their own right. At the request of publishers, artists produced series of prints immortalising famous locations of Japanese cities and provinces (*meisho-e*). In their views representing these picturesque sites, they captured the immense diversity of landscapes (winding rivers, verdant plains, wooded hills, etc.) in a variety of lights, depicting profusions of flowers, plants and animals. The artists highlighted the majesty and beauty of springtime nature, its renewed energy after winter, including in urban scenes. Thus, in the extensive series published by Utagawa Hiroshige towards the end of his life, *One Hundred Famous Views of Edo* (1856–1858), prints are arranged by season. Springtime by far contains the greatest number of views (forty-two plates), testifying to the artist's desire to depict the capital city in its most attractive light. Hiroshige indeed offered a poetic vision, idyllic even, enriched by the awakening of nature, honoured by the townsfolk with festivities and walks in the parks under the blossoming trees (pl. 15, 16, 20, 21, 23).

Hiroshige often opted for photographic framing, a particularly innovative type of composition, depicting features of plant life (flowers or branches) in the foreground, in front of the view of the landscape (pl. 29, 30, 32, 37, 38, 57, 71, 72) – an approach that would later be embraced by photographers. Among the masters of *ukiyo-e*, Hiroshige was undoubtedly the one who attached the greatest importance to spring. He indeed depicted this season in a multitude of works featuring the flowering of cherry and plum trees, the tender green shades of fresh grass and new leaves, the flight or melodious song of birds, the onset of a passing shower or a light breeze, the rising mist and the springtime ballet of insects – butterflies fluttering from flower to flower, or bees gathering nectar. In his relationship with nature, Hiroshige expressed a poetic sensibility – at times melancholic and nostalgic, with the sudden fall of flowers symbolising the brevity of life, and at other times joyful, with the gentle warmth of the air inviting viewers to enjoy walks and fleeting outdoor pleasures, to play games, to drink sake, to dance and to sing to melodies played on a *shamisen*, in a festive atmosphere.

Mono no aware (aesthetics and emotions inspired by the ephemeral beauty of nature)

The aesthetic concept of *mono no aware* reflects this awareness of life's fleeting moments and this invitation to seize the brief moments of happiness inspired by emotions born of the contemplation of the ephemeral beauty of nature. This acute perception of nature, graced with acute melancholic sensibility, is imbued with Buddhist spirituality, inspired by the notion that all things are impermanent; it encourages us viewers to enjoy the moments of pleasure that the natural environment awakens within us. Suzuki Harunobu illustrates this, with the young woman gathering flowers near a river waterfall (pl. 48).

To capture these springtime sensations and the changing impressions of a "floating, moving world" (*ukiyo*), Hiroshige utilised all the technical resources offered by coloured woodcuts, alternately using bright hues and gradients to render the ephemeral world evoked by Asai Ryōi in 1661 in *Tales of the Floating World* (*Ukiyo monogatari*): "Living only for the moment,

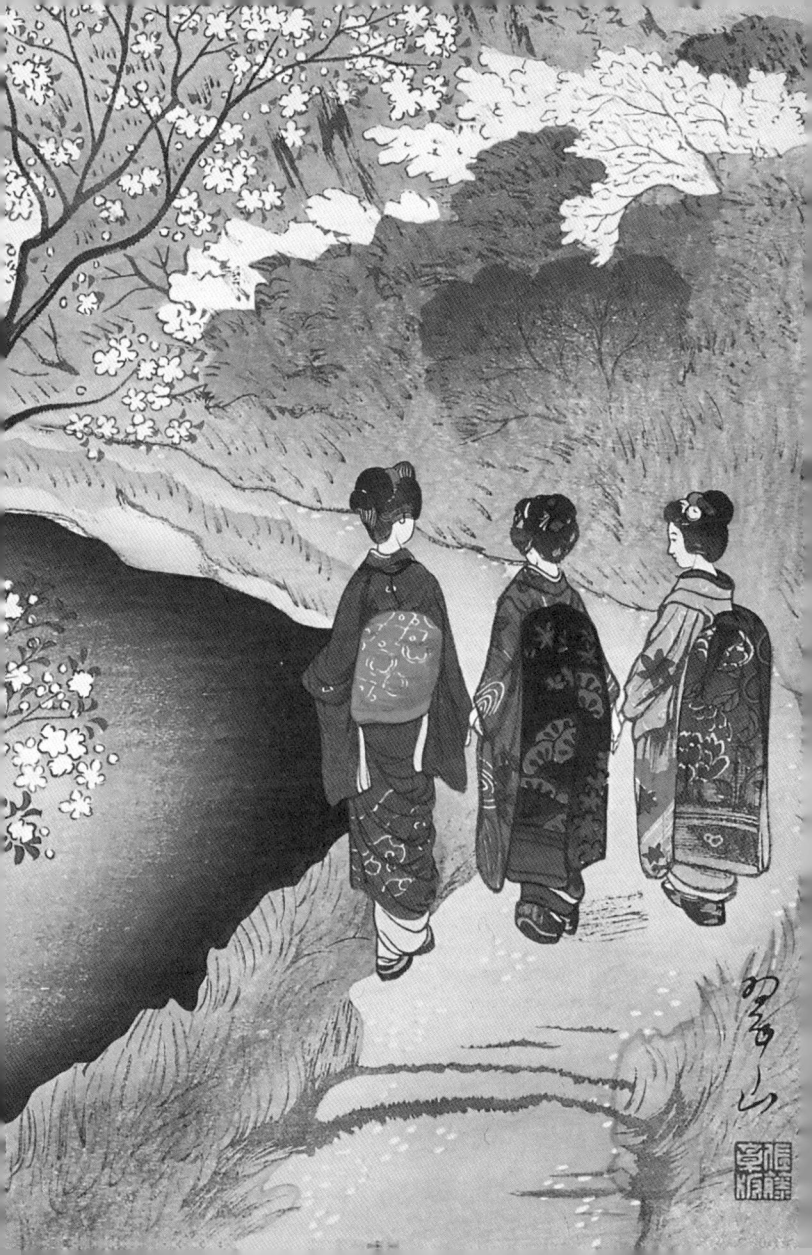

savouring the moon, the snow, the cherry blossoms, and the maple leaves, singing songs, drinking wine, and diverting oneself in simply floating, unconcerned by the prospect of imminent poverty, buoyant and carefree, like a gourd carried along with the current of the river: this is what we call *ukiyo* [the floating world]." Paying particular attention to fluctuations in light, atmospheric phenomena, climatic variations and the beauty of nature, Hiroshige lyrically evoked springtime and its procession of ephemeral, cyclical manifestations, enthusiastically observing the season's incessant changes; the mastery with which he recreated atmospheric effects, shifting sensations, the present moment and the impression of a fleeting moment made him a precursor of the Impressionists. Thus, in *Ōiso: Tora's Rain* (the 45th station of the Tōkaidō, pl. 34), he seized the ephemeral moment of the onset of a spring shower, contrasting the clarity of the ocean, calm and bathed in sunlight in the background, with the darkness of the foreground, where travellers are surprised by the first raindrops. He immersed natural and picturesque locations of Japan in a mysterious atmosphere, depicting them realistically and identifiably, while also imbuing them with a poetic aura, often suggesting a moment of the day: a misty dawn (pl. 4, 12), dawn and sunrise (pl. 22), dusk and sunset (pl. 5, 6, 13, 15, 16, 21, 22), a night illuminated by moonlight (pl. 1), and more.

Kacho-ga (flowers and birds)

The season of springtime is also reflected in the classic Chinese-born theme of *kacho-ga* – the art of depicting flowers and birds, whose fragile beauty highlights the vulnerability of life and the transience of all pleasures. Introduced to Japan as early as the fourteenth century, where it is mentioned by name in an inventory of paintings drawn up by Buddhist monks, this genre was then embraced by *ukiyo-e* artists in the eighteenth century, appearing only marginally in prints and books. Here, plants suggest a particular season – for instance, cherry or plum blossoms for springtime, peonies for summer, maple trees for autumn and pine trees for winter. Colour printing encouraged a trend towards naturalism, while interest in the natural sciences, particularly botany, flourished. In the album *Selected Insects* (*Ehon mushi erami*, 1788), Kitagawa Utamaro illustrates a selection of *kyōka* (parody poems), combining a selection flowers and plants with a variety of insects, such as the impressively realistic butterflies and dragonfly (pl. 47). Plants, birds and insects are also frequently featured on *surimono* (refined greetings cards).

In the early 1830s, Katsushika Hokusai published a series of large prints depicting flowers and birds in vertical format. Among the large birds, waders and birds of prey that he captured in prints at different seasons of the year, for springtime, he chose a hawk, standing proudly on its perch in front of blossoming plum trees (pl. 44). With finesse and precision, he also depicted a plant associated with spring and fertility: a lively bundle of irises (pl. 58). On this print, he detailed the veins and fine tears of the long green leaves and the delicacy of the flower's colourful orange petals, flecked with blue and violet. In Japan, irises have a rich symbolic value and are celebrated in May. They are also associated with virility, with the shape of the leaves recalling the blade of a *katana*, the traditional samurai sword. Hokusai depicted a large grasshopper devouring the uppermost leaf, maybe symbolically suggesting the triumph of the merchant class over dwindling feudalism.

Like Utagawa Toyohiro, the master who trained him, Utagawa Hiroshige also excelled in the art of depicting plants and animals. He produced a large number of prints of flowers and birds (some two hundred studies, often produced in a narrow vertical format), contributed to *kacho-ga*'s rise to fame from the 1830s onwards, and gradually conquered the market for this type of print, which was very popular with the public. His observations of flora and fauna are almost scientific in their truth and precision, worthy of a naturalist; however, they are not devoid of poetry and lyricism. Hiroshige's aesthetic approach was simple and focused on the essentials, following the tradition of the haiku, short seventeen-syllable poems that often accompany his *kacho-ga*, evoking the sensations of the season. With remarkable meticulousness and skill, he analysed the supple, graceful movements of birds, drawing them in full flight or perched on a branch: the swallow (pl. 70), the sparrow (pl. 26, 28, 54, 69), the Java sparrow (pl. 45, 68), the canary (pl. 64), the oriole (pl. 19), the kingfisher (pl. 40) and others. In his prints, these birds appear in perfect harmony with the surrounding flora: hibiscus, mimosa, camellia, clematis, wisteria, viburnum, cherry and plum blossoms, and more. In Hiroshige's compositions, in the distance, a flight of wild geese sometimes enlivens the sky above Mount Fuji (pl. 21), a sunset (pl. 8) or a plain where the vegetation is moved by the wind (pl. 75).

His pupil Shigenobu, who took the name Hiroshige II, produced some superb prints devoted to flowers, notably in his series *Thirty-six Selected Flowers*. These prints include mimosas (pl. 29), clovers (pl. 30), bellflowers (pl. 32), pear blossoms (pl. 37), primroses (pl. 38) and narcissus (pl. 72). This tradition of *kacho-ga* was perpetuated in the Meiji era by painters such as Watanabe Shōtei (pl. 28), and in the 20th century by the *shin-hanga* movement and artists such as Hasui Kawase (pl. 71), Chigusa Soun (pl. 49, 50) and Shodo Kawarazaki (pl. 25, 36, 51, 57, 60, 74).

Hanami (the contemplation of cherry blossoms)

The celebration of spring culminates in the traditional *Hanami* Festival, the "contemplation of cherry blossoms". This fruit tree, the *Sakura*, whose blossoms can take on any shade of pink, has become the emblem of Japan. For a few days, the country is resplendent with subtle, delicate shades of pink. Every year, in the early spring, the ancestral ritual of *Hanami* (which originally heralded the rice-planting season) offers an occasion to enjoy walks in the countryside and the city and picnics under the trees (pl. 2, 8, 23). In the company of family or friends, Japan's residents can admire this brief and marvellous flowering, which rarely lasts more than ten days or so. The fleeting beauty of this full bloom is followed by the abrupt fall of the flowers, whose petals then scatter throughout valleys, covering plains and floating down rivers (pl. 33).

In honour of this custom, countless prints showcase the beauty of this flowering and the delicacy of the cherry blossom petals (pl. 1 to 24). Planted along roadsides, adorning the edges of shrines and lining the banks of rivers, cherry trees are found everywhere throughout the country. In the *39th View of Mount Fuji*, Katsushika Hokusai depicts city dwellers, travellers and samurai strolling along the Tōkaidō road, on a hillside near Edo, under cherry trees covered with splendid pale pink blossoms. A group of people are picnicking and enjoying a drink of sake at the top of a hill, from which they can contemplate a magnificent view of Mount Fuji (pl. 2). Hiroshige also depicted the tradition of picnicking under cherry blossom trees during *Hanami*, particularly in the large park on the verdant Asuka Hill in Edo, which also offers a superb view of Mount Fuji (pl. 8).

In this way, the masters of Japanese printmaking pay poetic tribute to springtime, depicting it as a metaphor for life, both luminous and beautiful, yet also fleeting and ephemeral. The themes and style of *ukiyo-e* perfectly embody this season; the vivid hues, rich colours and subtle gradients that characterise these prints help recreate the sensations of spring, magnifying the awakening of wildlife, the multicoloured blossoming of flowers adorning landscapes, the shifting light and the vibrant reflections that bathe the atmosphere.

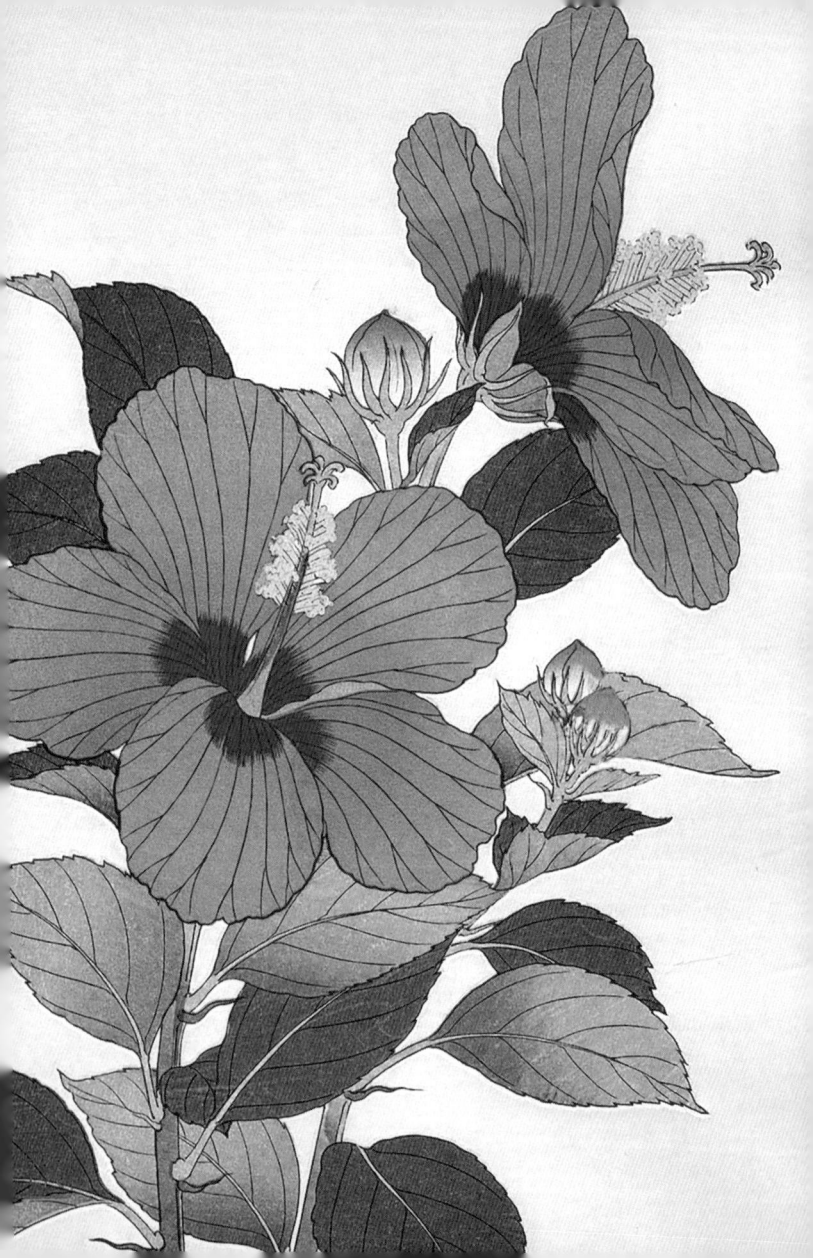

The great masters of printmaking
presented in this book

Suzuki HARUNOBU (1724–1770)

Komai GENKI, (alias KOMAI KI) (1747–1797)

Kitagawa UTAMARO (ca. 1753–1806)

Katsushika HOKUSAI (1760–1849)

Teisai HOKUBA (1771–1844)

Utagawa KUNISADA I (alias Utagawa Toyokuni III) (1786–1865)

Utagawa HIROSHIGE (1797–1858)

Utagawa KUNIYOSHI (1798–1861)

Utagawa KUNISADA II (1823–1880)

Utagawa HIROSHIGE II (alias Shigenobu) (1826–1869)

Toyohara KUNICHIKA (1835–1900)

Kobayashi Kiyochika (1847–1915)

Watanabe SHŌTEI (1851–1918)

Mizuno TOSHIKATA (1866–1908)

Chigusa SOUN (1873–1944)

Hasui KAWASE (1883–1957)

Miki SUIZAN (1887–1957)

Shodo KAWARAZAKI (1889–1973)

Kasamatsu SHIRŌ (1898–1991)

Captions of previous pages

pp. 4–5
Utagawa Hiroshige
Evening Glow at Koganei Border, 1837–1838 (detail, pl. 6)

p. 6
Utagawa Kuniyoshi
Spring, ca. 1843 (detail, pl. 27)

pp. 8–9
Suzuki Harunobu
A Bijin or beautiful woman picking flowers by a river, ca. 1765 (detail, pl. 48)

p. 13
Miki Suizan
Three girls strolling at Arashiyama, ca. 1924 (detail, pl. 17)

p. 18
Shodo Kawarazaki
Pink Hibiscus, ca. 1950 (detail, pl. 36)

Opposite page
Utagawa Hiroshige II, alias Shigenobu
Mimosa at the Ayase River in Tokyo, 1866 (detail, pl. 29)

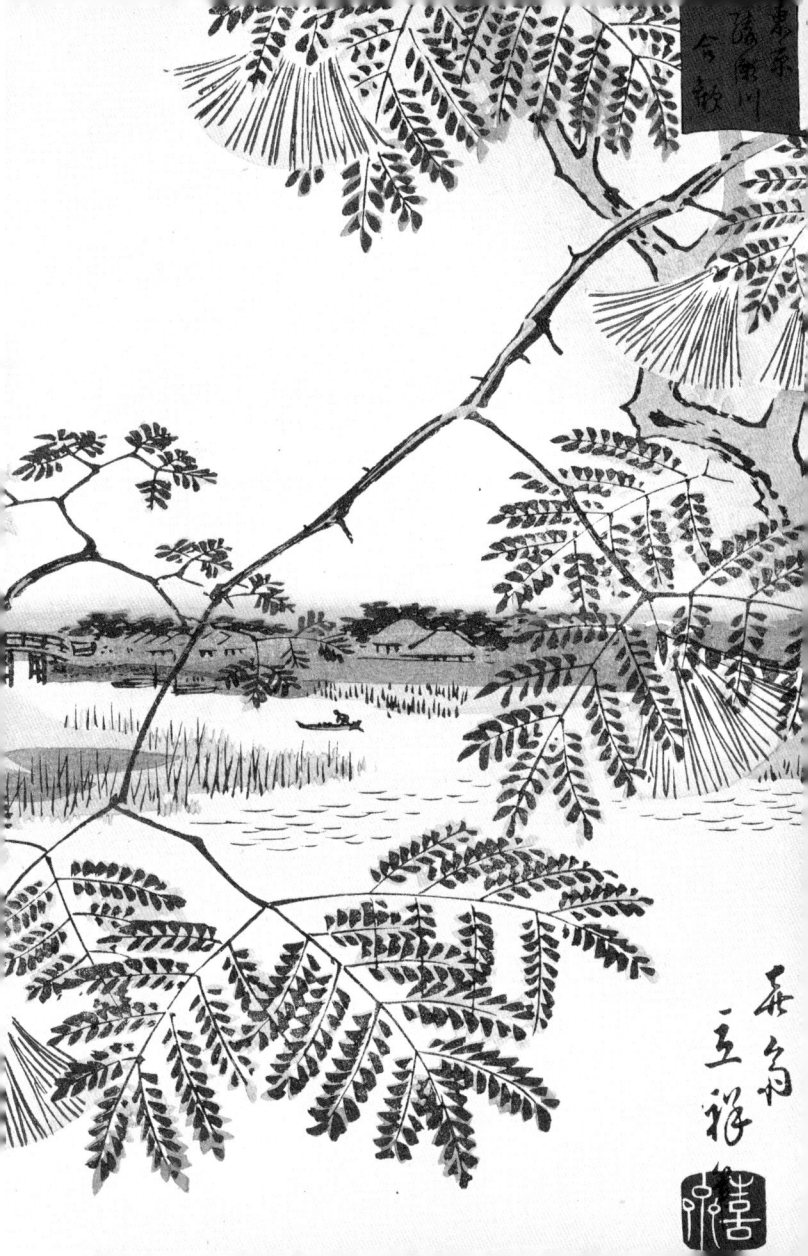

1| Utagawa Hiroshige
Evening Cherry on Mt. Yoshino
ca. 1830–1840
22 × 35.5 cm

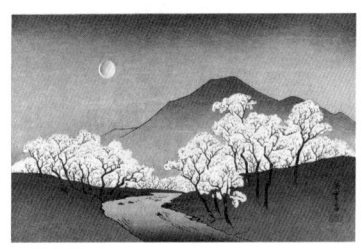

2| Katsushika Hokusai
Fuji from Gotenyama
at Shinagawa on the Tōkaidō
From the series: *Thirty-six Views of*
Mount Fuji, pl. 39, ca. 1830–1832
26.7 × 38.8 cm

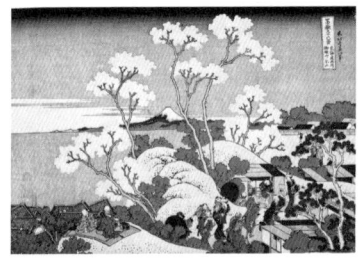

3| Katsushika Hokusai
Poem by Gon-Chūnagon Masafusa
From the series: *One Hundred Poems*
Explained by the Nurse, ca. 1835
24.8 × 37.1 cm

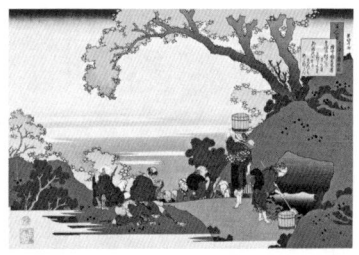

4| Utagawa Hiroshige
Chiyogaike Pond, Meguro
From the series: *One Hundred
Famous Views of Edo*, pl. 23, 1856
36.5 × 24.5 cm

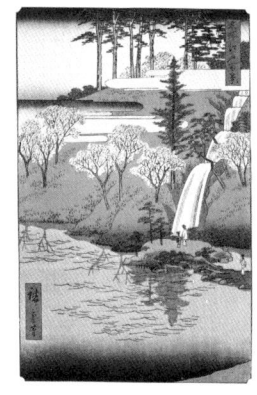

5| Utagawa Hiroshige
*The Dam on the Otonashi River at Ōji,
Commonly Called "The Great Waterfall"*
From the series: *One Hundred
Famous Views of Edo*, pl. 19, 1857
36.5 × 24.5 cm

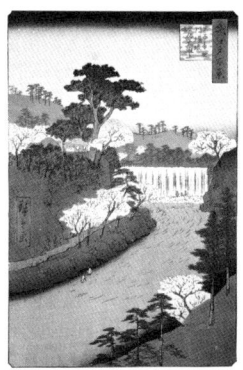

6| Utagawa Hiroshige
Evening Glow at Koganei Border
1837–1838
25.1 × 36.2 cm

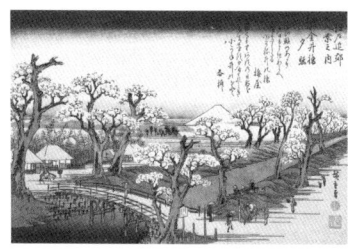

7| Utagawa Hiroshige
The Embankment at Koganei in Musashi
From the series: *Thirty-six Views of*
Mount Fuji (horizontal format)
pl. 33, 1852
18.3 × 25 cm

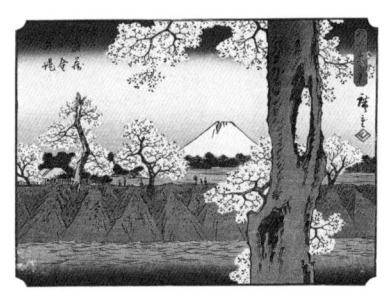

8| Utagawa Hiroshige
Asuka Hill in the Eastern Capital
From the series: *Thirty-six Views*
of Mount Fuji (horizontal format)
pl. 22, 1852
18.3 × 25 cm

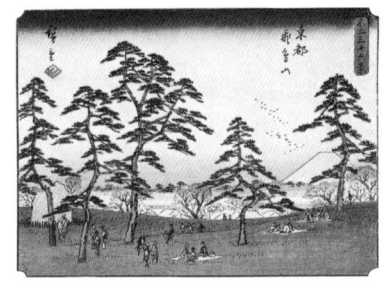

9| Utagawa Hiroshige
Yoshitsune's Cherry Tree and
the Shrine to Noriyori at Ishiyakushi
From the series: *The Fifty-three*
Stations of the Tōkaidō, pl. 45, 1855
36 × 23 cm

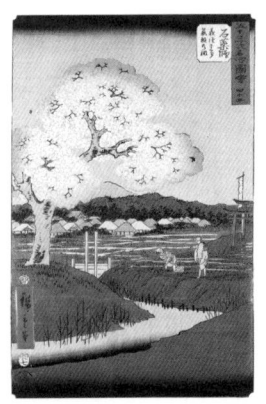

10| Utagawa Hiroshige
Asuka Hill in the Eastern Capital
From the series: *Thirty-six Views of*
Mount Fuji (vertical format),
pl. 8, ca. 1858
35.8 × 23.5 cm

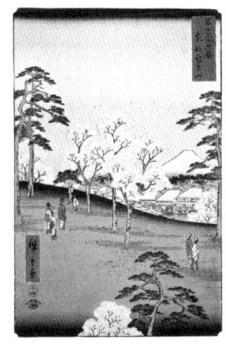

11| Utagawa Hiroshige
Kiyomizu Hall and Shinobazu Pond
at Ueno From the series: *One Hundred*
Famous Views of Edo, pl. 11, 1856
36.3 × 25.5 cm

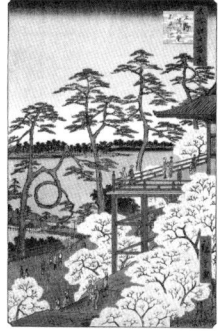

12| Utagawa Hiroshige
Sendagi Dangozaka
From the series: *One Hundred*
Famous Views of Edo, pl. 16, 1856
36.3 × 24.3 cm

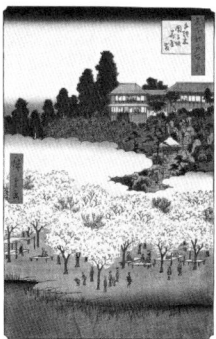

13| Utagawa Hiroshige
Moto-Hachiman Shrine, Sunamura
From the series: *One Hundred*
Famous Views of Edo, pl. 29, 1856
36.3 × 25.5 cm

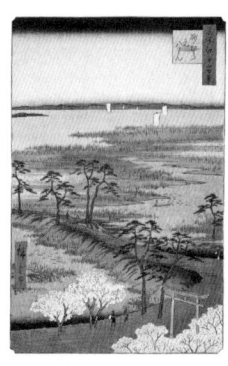

14| Utagawa Hiroshige
Blossoms on the Tama River Embankment
From the series: *One Hundred*
Famous Views of Edo, pl. 42, 1856
36 × 25 cm

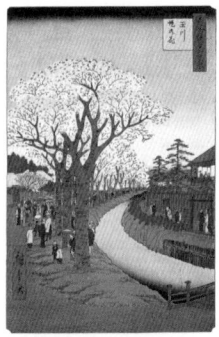

15| Utagawa Hiroshige
Plum Garden at Kamata
From the series: *One Hundred*
Famous Views of Edo, pl. 27, 1857
36.3 × 24.4 cm

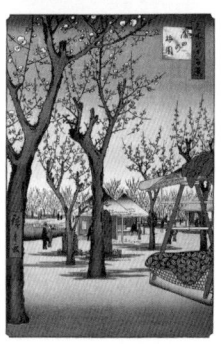

16| Utagawa Hiroshige
Plum Garden at Kameido
From the series: *One Hundred
Famous Views of Edo*, pl. 30, 1857
36 × 24.4 cm

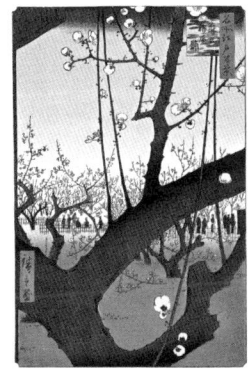

17| Miki Suizan
Spring at Arashiyama
From the series: *New Selection
of Noted Places of Kyoto*, 1924
27.8 × 39.5 cm

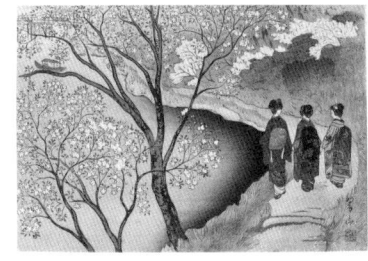

**18| Utagawa Kunisada alias
Utagawa Toyokuni III**
Women Walking in Spring Garden
ca. 1830
35.3 × 23.9 cm

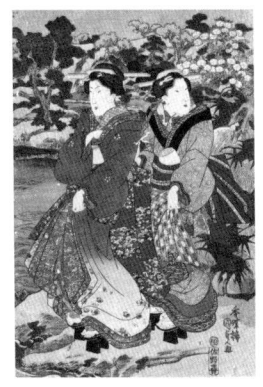

19| **Utagawa Hiroshige**
Hibiscus and Black-naped Oriole
ca. 1830
37.5 × 13 cm

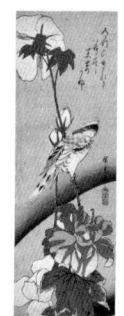

20| **Utagawa Hiroshige**
Temple Gardens, Nippori
From the series: *One Hundred
Famous Views of Edo*, pl. 14, 1857
36 × 24 cm

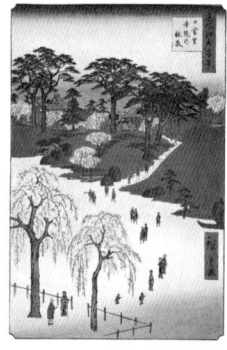

21| **Utagawa Hiroshige**
Azuma Shrine and the Entwined Camphor
From the series: *One Hundred
Famous Views of Edo*, pl. 31, 1856
35.9 × 24 cm

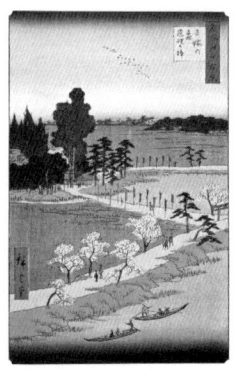

22| Utagawa Hiroshige
Sunrise At Kanda Myōjin Shrine
From the series: *One Hundred
Famous Views of Edo*, pl. 10, 1857
33.7 × 22.2 cm

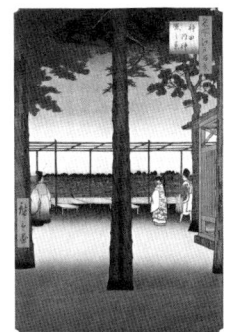

23| Utagawa Hiroshige
View to the North from Asuka Hill
From the series: *One Hundred
Famous Views of Edo*, pl. 17, 1856
35.9 × 24.1 cm

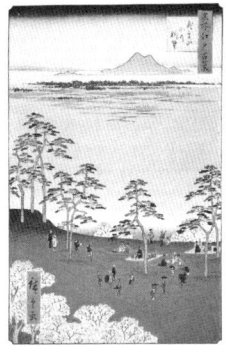

24| Utagawa Hiroshige
*The Outskirts of Koshigaya in
Musashi Province*
From the series: *Thirty-six Views
of Mount Fuji* (vertical format),
pl. 14, ca. 1858
36.2 × 24.8 cm

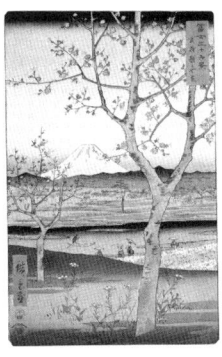

25 | Shodo Kawarazaki
Boke (Japanese Quince)
ca. 1950
36.5 × 23.8 cm

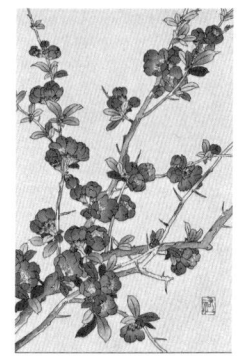

26 | Teisai Hokuba
Marsh-tits and Crab Apple Flowers
From the series: *Spring Rain
Collection*, vol. 3, ca. 1820
18.7 × 20.3 cm

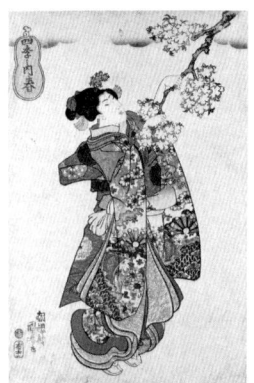

27 | Utagawa Kuniyoshi
Spring
From the series: *Women's Pleasures
of the Four Seasons*, ca. 1843
35.6 × 23.8 cm

28| Watanabe Shōtei
Bird on a branch of flowering tree
n.a., 21 × 27.5 cm

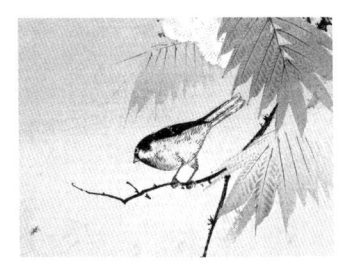

29| Utagawa Hiroshige II,
alias Shigenobu
Mimosa at the Ayase River in Tokyo
From the series: *Thirty-six*
Selected Flowers 1866
36 × 23.5 cm

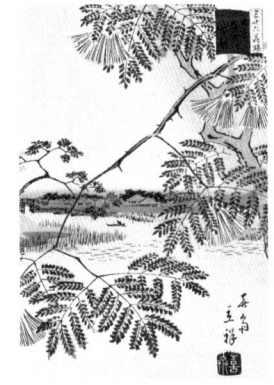

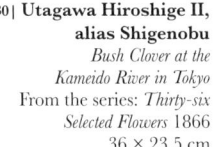

30| Utagawa Hiroshige II,
alias Shigenobu
Bush Clover at the
Kameido River in Tokyo
From the series: *Thirty-six*
Selected Flowers 1866
36 × 23.5 cm

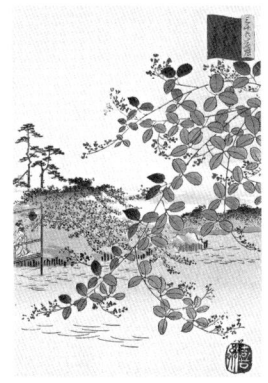

31| Utagawa Hiroshige
Basho's Hermitage and Camellia Hill
on the Kanda Aqueduct at Sekiguchi
From the series: *One Hundred*
Famous Views of Edo, pl. 40, 1857
35.5 × 24.3 cm

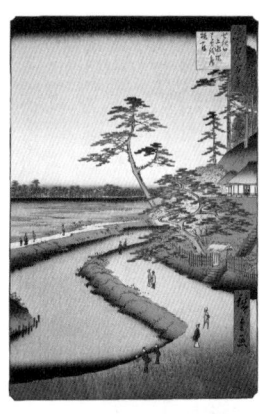

32| Utagawa Hiroshige II,
alias Shigenobu
Bellflowers at Hiroo Plain in Tokyo
From the series: *Thirty-six*
Selected Flowers, 1866
36 × 23.5 cm

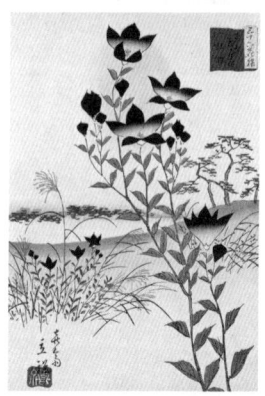

33| Utagawa Hiroshige
Cherry Blossoms at Arashiyama
ca. 1834
22 × 35.4 cm

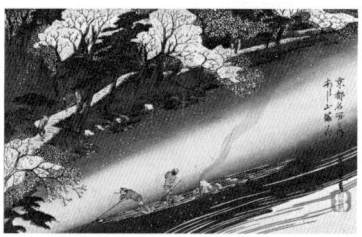

34| Utagawa Hiroshige
Ōiso: Tora's Rain
From the series: *The Fifty-three*
Stations of the Tōkaidō, 45th station
1833–1834
22.2 × 34.4 cm

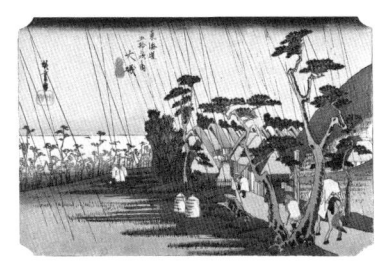

35| Kobayashi Kiyochika
A Mountain behind Sanno Shrine
and Paulownia
From the series: *One Hundred*
Famous Views of Musashi, ca. 1884
37.2 × 25 cm

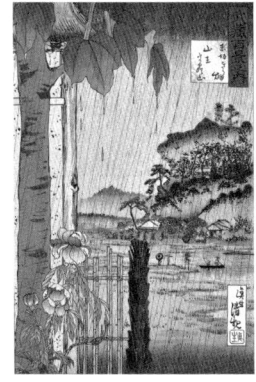

36| Shodo Kawarazaki
Hibiscus
ca. 1950
36.5 × 23.8 cm

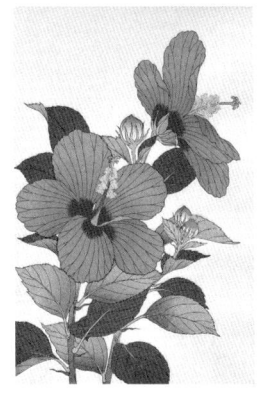

**37| Utagawa Hiroshige II,
alias Shigenobu**
Pear Blossoms at Rokuroku in the Eastern Capital
From the series: *Thirty-six Selected Flowers*
1866
36 × 23.5 cm

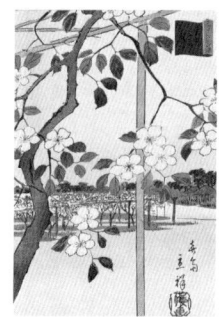

**38| Utagawa Hiroshige II,
alias Shigenobu**
Primrose at Todahara in Tokyo
From the series: *Thirty-six Selected Flowers*
1866
36 × 23.5 cm

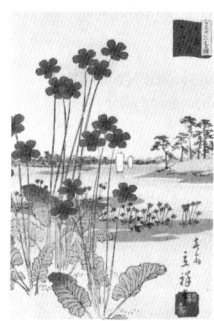

39| Utagawa Hiroshige
Kingfisher and Viburnum
1840–1849
34.7 × 11.5 cm

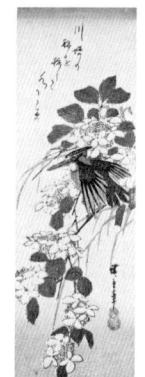

40 | Komai Genki, alias Komai Ki
Chinese Beauty Beside a Plum Tree
Album: *A Contest of Beauties from
the Near and Distant Past*, published
by Aoki Kosaburo
in Osaka, ca. 1780–1790
(reprinted 1895)
21.6 × 13.5 cm

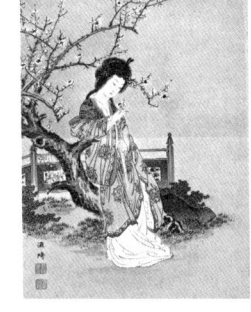

41 | Utagawa Kunisada II
*Narcissus, Winter Camellia
and Plum Blossoms in Cold*
From the series: *A Collection of Flowers
for the Modern Genji*, 1861
Triptych: 35.4 × 73.7 cm
(detail from the right-hand side)

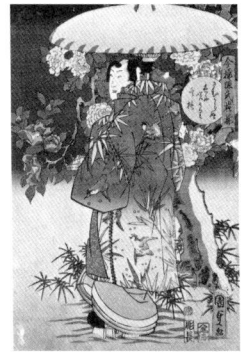

42 | Utagawa Kunisada II
*Narcissus, Winter Camellia
and Plum Blossoms in Cold*
From the series: *A Collection of Flowers
for the Modern Genji*, 1861
Triptych: 35.4 × 73.7 cm
(detail from the left-hand side)

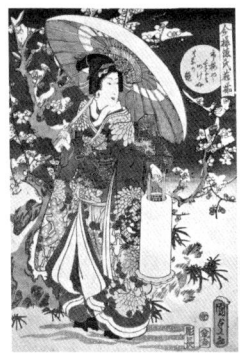

43| Utagawa Kuniyoshi
Poem by Sakyō no Dayū Michimasa
From the series: *One Hundred Poems
by One Hundred Poets*, ca. 1840–1842
38 × 26.1 cm

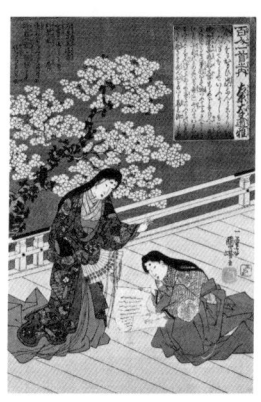

44| Katsushika Hokusai
Hawk and Cherry Blossoms
From the series: *Bird-and-Flower
Paintings*, 1833–1834
52 × 23.1 cm

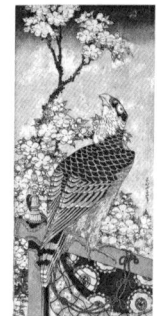

45| Katsushika Hokusai
Finches and Cherry Blossoms
From the series: *Bird-and-Flower
Paintings*, ca. 1816–1820
36.7 × 25.6 cm

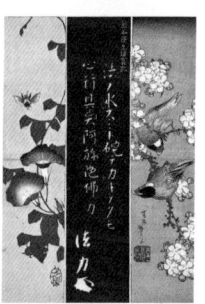

46| Toyohara Kunichika
*Spring Sake Party amid
the Blossoms with a Woman*
1862
36.7 × 25.6 cm
(left-hand part of a triptych)

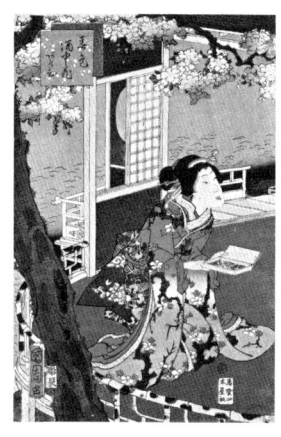

47| Kitagawa Utamaro
Butterfly and Dragonfly
Album: *Picture Book of Selected
Insects*, 1788
18.4 × 26.7 cm

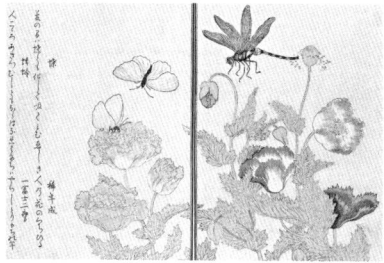

48| Suzuki Harunobu
*A Bijin or beautiful woman
picking flowers by a river*
ca. 1765
19 × 25 cm

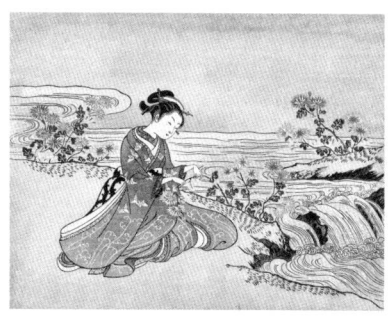

49 | Chigusa Soun
Hollyhock
1900, 43 × 27.3 cm

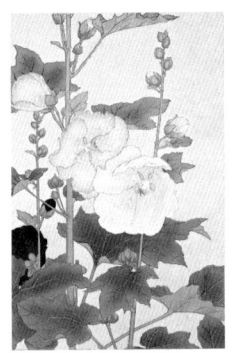

50 | Chigusa Soun
Poppy
1900
43 × 27.3 cm

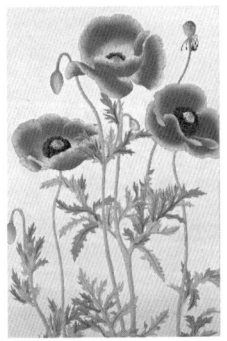

51 | Shodo Kawarazaki
Pink Morning Glories
From the series: *Floral Calendar*
of Japan 1951
36.5 × 23.8 cm

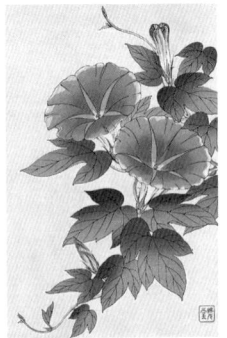

52| Utagawa Kuniyoshi
Woman and Girl Picking Flowers
From the series: *A Collection of Songs Set to Koto Music*, 1840
37 × 24.9 cm

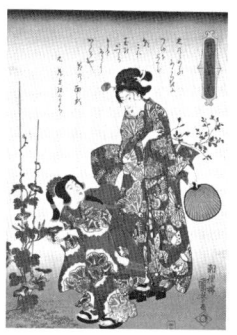

53| Utagawa Kunisada alias Utagawa Toyokuni III
Flowers
From the series: *Snow, Moon and Flowers*, ca. 1847–1852
Triptych: 36.4 × 76.2 cm
(detail from the central panel)

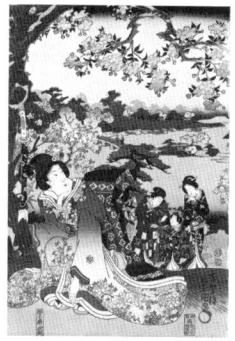

54| Utagawa Hiroshige
Tit and Peony
ca. 1830
18.7 × 12.4 cm

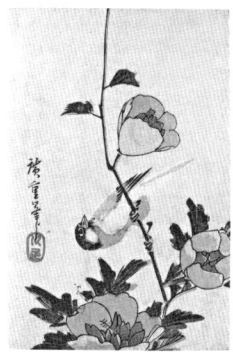

**55| Utagawa Kunisada
alias Utagawa Toyokuni III**
*Viewing Cherry Blossoms
in the Palace Garden in Spring*
ca. 1847–1852
Triptych: 37.5 × 76.2 cm

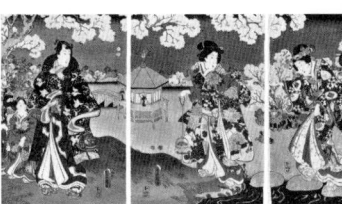

56| Utagawa Hiroshige
In the Kameido Tenjin Shrine Compound
From the series: *One Hundred
Famous Views of Edo*, pl. 65, 1856
36.5 × 24.5 cm

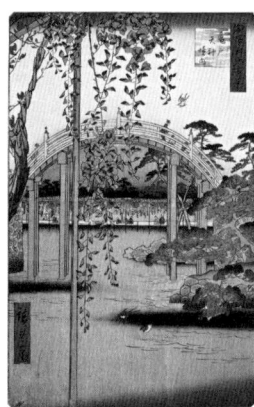

57| Shodo Kawarazaki
Wisteria
From the series:
Floral Calendar of Japan
1951
41 × 27 cm

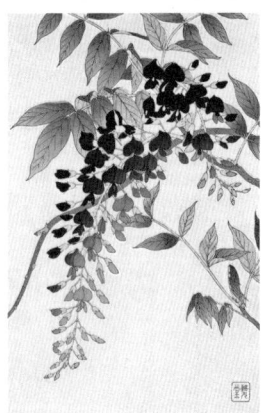

58| Kasushika Hokusai
Grasshopper and Iris
From the series: *Large Flowers*
ca. 1830–1834
25.2 × 36.5 cm

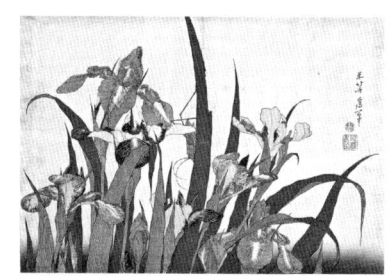

59| Mizuno Toshikata
Courtesan and Attendant.
House of Pleasure: Woman
of the Meiwa Era
From the series: *Thirty-six*
Elegant Selections ca. 1891–1893
35.6 × 24 cm

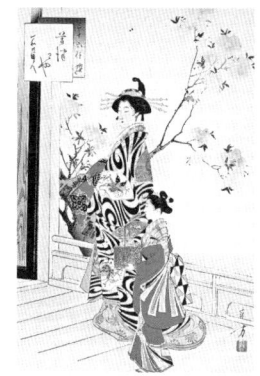

60| Shodo Kawarazaki
Azalea
From the series: *Floral Calendar*
of Japan 1951
41 × 27 cm

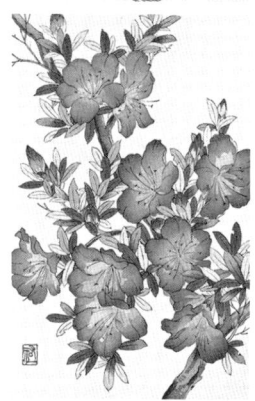

61| Utagawa Kuniyoshi
*The Tama River
in Musashi Province*
ca. 1847, Each plate of the
triptych: 26 × 37.8 cm

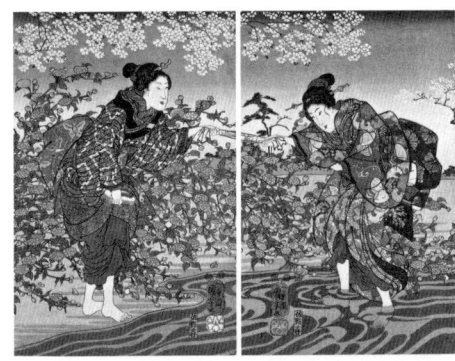

**62| Utagawa Kunisada alias
Utagawa Toyokuni III**
*Outside a Brushwood Fence
on a Spring Night*
ca. 1847–1852
Triptych: 36.3 × 75 cm

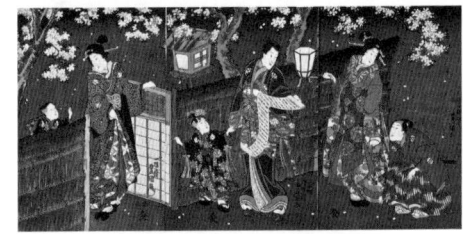

63| Suzuki Harunobu
*Woman Admiring Plum
Blossoms at Night*
ca. 1766
32.4 × 21 cm

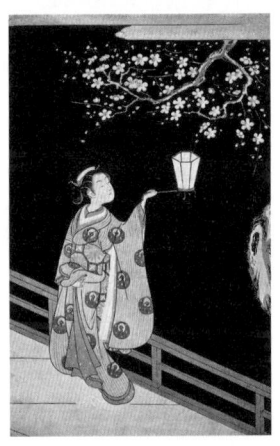

64 | Utagawa Hiroshige
Canary and camellias
ca. 1840–1849
35.4 × 11.9 cm

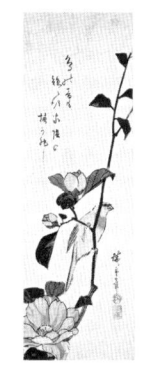

65 | Suzuki Harunobu
Hagi
From the series: *Beauties of the Floating World Compared to Flowers*
ca. 1770
27.7 × 19.2 cm

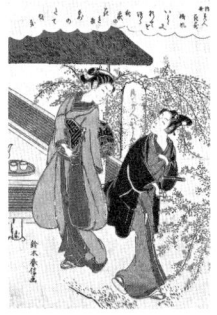

66 | Utagawa Hiroshige
Red Blossom Plum
ca. 1843–1847
34.8 × 11.3 cm

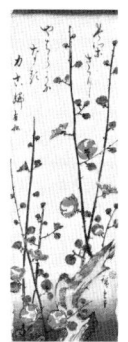

67 | Suzuki Harunobu
Lovers on a Veranda with a Shamisen
ca. 1760
19 × 25 cm

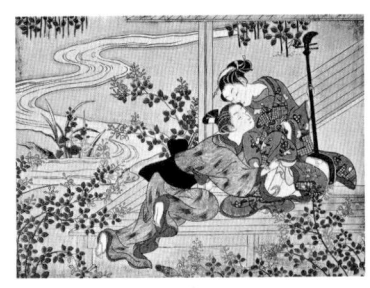

68 | Utagawa Hiroshige
Java Sparrow and Clematis
1830–1839
34.3 × 11.4 (right)

69 | Utagawa Hiroshige
Sparrow and Clematis
1842–1857
34.6 × 11.3 cm (left)

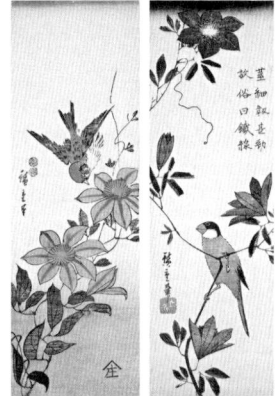

70 | Utagawa Hiroshige
Swallow, Yellow Bird and Wisteria
ca. 1830–1849
26.5 × 18.9 cm

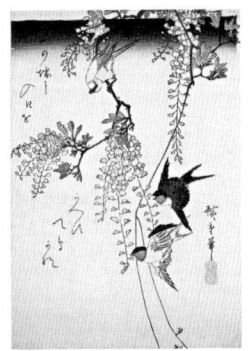

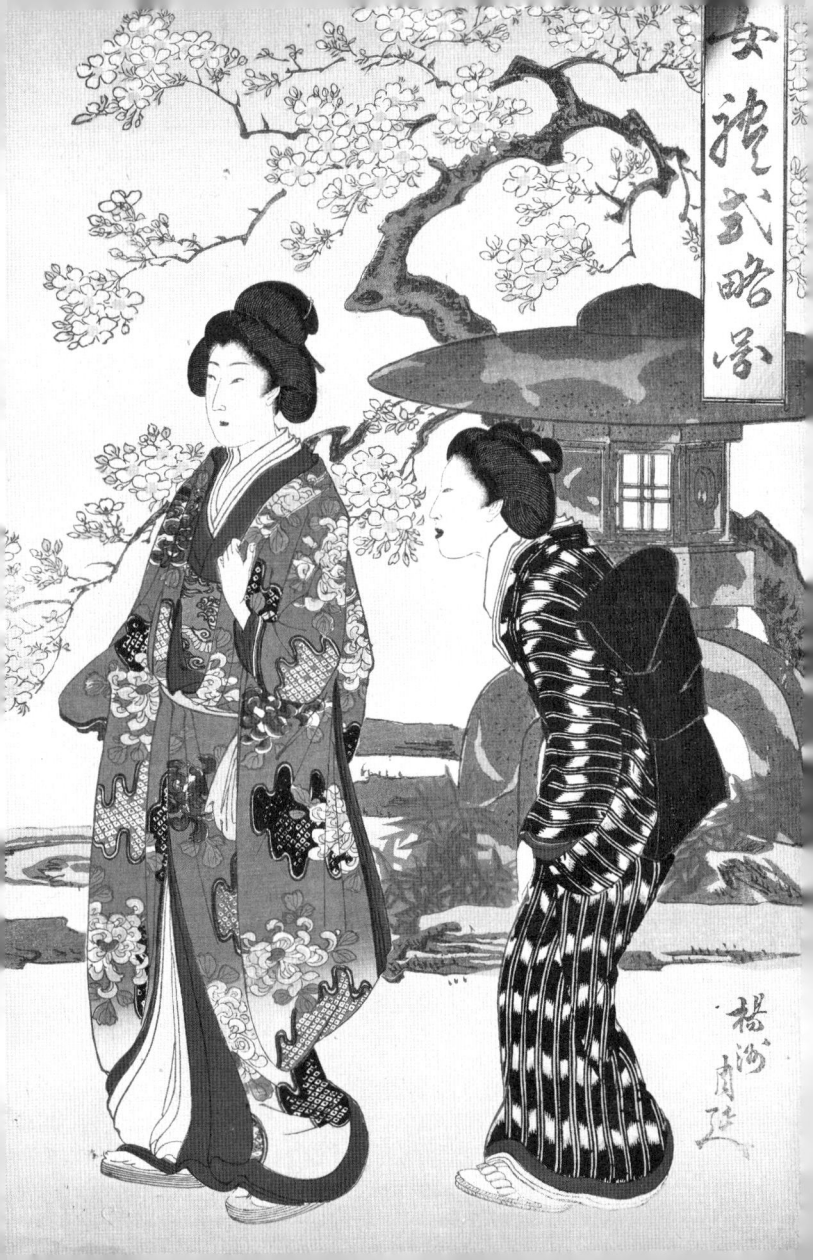

Photographic credits

The numbers refer to those of the images reproduced in this booklet.

Art Institute of Chicago / Clarence Buckingham Collection: 2, 5, 11, 13, 16, 21, 24, 39, 64, 68, 69, 70; / Bruce Goff Archive, gift of Shin'enkan, Inc.: 3, 4, 14; / Gift of Dr. and Mrs. Maurice H. Cottle: 10; / Frederick W. Gookin Collection: 12, 15, 22, 23, 31; / Gift of Mr. and Mrs. Harold G. Henderson: 20, 56

Bridgeman Images: 41, 42; / Photograph © 2023 Museum of Fine Arts, Boston. All rights reserved: 18, 29, 32, 37, 38, 52, 53, 55, 62, 65, 72; / Pictures from History: 48

Fuji Arts: 51, 57, 60

Harvard Art Museums / Arthur M. Sackler Museum, Gift of Dr. Denman W. Ross: 1

Japanese Art Open Database: 17; / Rogers Fund, 1918: 34, 74

Minneapolis Institute of Art / Gift of Louis W. Hill, Jr.: 33; / Bequest of Richard P. Gale: 58; / Gift of Gary L. Gliem: 71; / Gift of Ellen and Fred Wells: 73

Rhode Island School of Design Museum: 44, 54

Rijksmuseum, Amsterdam: 61

Sakura Fine Art: 25

Scholten Japanese Art: 35

Syracuse University Art Museum / Gift of Mr. Hamilton Armstrong: 28

The Metropolitan Museum of Art, New York / Henry L. Phillips Collection, Bequest of Henry L. Phillips, 1939: 6; / The Howard Mansfield Collection, Purchase, Rogers Fund, 1936: 19, 47; / H. O. Havemeyer Collection, Bequest of Mrs. H. O. Havemeyer, 1929: 26, 45; / Gift of Donald Keene, in honor of Julia Meech-Pekarik, 1986: 40; / Gift of Mr. and Mrs. Malcolm P. Aldrich, 1984: 59; / Fletcher Fund, 1929: 63; / The Howard Mansfield Collection, Purchase, Rogers Fund, 1936: 66

Tokyo Metro Library: 30

University of Wisconsin – Madison / Chazen Museum of Art / Bequest of John H. Van Vleck: 7, 75; / Bequest of Abigail Van Vleck: 9

© Prestel Verlag, Munich · London
New York, 2026
1st edition 2026

Prestel Verlag
A member of Penguin Random House
Verlagsgruppe GmbH
Neumarkter Straße 28 · 81673 Munich

produktsicherheit@penguinrandomhouse.de
(The above information is mandatory information
according to GPSR and should be used for all
queries relating to the safety of our books)

The publisher expressly reserves the right to
exploit the copyrighted content of this work
for the purposes of text and data mining in
accordance with Section 44b of the German
Copyright Act (UrhG), based on the European
Digital Single Market Directive. Any unauthorised
use is an infringement of copyright and is hereby
prohibited.

A CIP catalogue record for this book is available
from the British Library.

The French original edition was published by
Édition Hazan as Le Printemps
© Editions Hazan, 2024

Translation
David Rocher

Proofreading
John Stilwell

Production
Martina Effaga

Typesetting
Weiß-Freiburg GmbH, Grafik & Buchgestaltung

Lithographie
Hyphen-Group, Orio al Serio, Italie, Italy

Printing and binding
Toppan Leefung Printing

Printed in China

Penguin Random House Verlagsgruppe
FSC® N001967

ISBN 978-3-7913-7797-1

www.prestel.com

74 | Shodo Kawarazaki
Hollyhock
From the series:
Floral Calendar of Japan 1951
36.5 × 23.8 cm

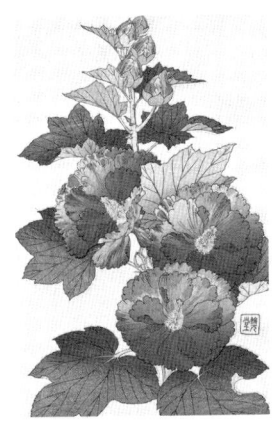

75 | Utagawa Hiroshige
Musashi Plain
From the series: *Thirty-six Views*
of Mount Fuji (horizontal format)
pl. 35, 1852
18.3 × 25 cm

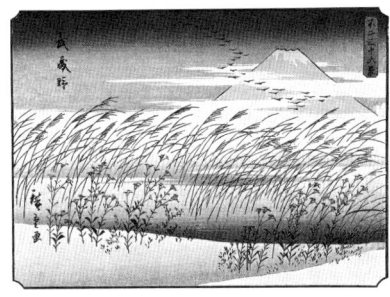

71 | Hasui Kawase
Spring in Arashiyama
April 1934
36.2 × 23.9 cm

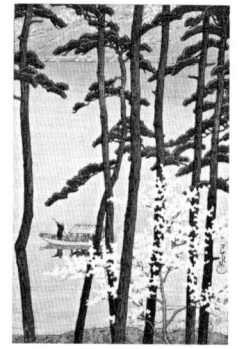

**72 | Utagawa Hiroshige II,
alias Shigenobu**
*Narcissus at Oshiage in the
Eastern Capital*
From the series: *Thirty-six
Selected Flowers*, 1866
36 × 23.5 cm

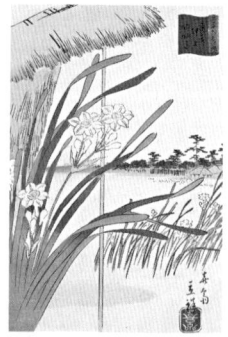

73 | Kasamatsu Shirō
Early Spring Tea Ceremony
1932
39.3 × 26.5 cm

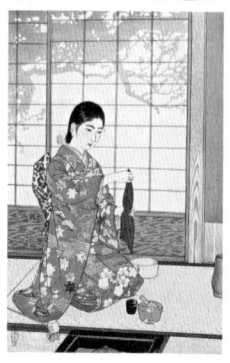